HERE COMES
GARFIELD

HERE COMES
GARFIELD

BY: JIM DAVIS

BALLANTINE BOOKS · NEW YORK

Copyright © 1982 by United Feature Syndicate, Inc. HERE COMES GARFIELD is based on the television special produced by United Media Productions. Jay Poynor, Executive Producer, in association with Lee Mendelson-Bill Melendez Productions, written by Jim Davis (© 1982 United Feature Syndicate, Inc.) All rights reserved under International and Pan-American Copyright Conventions. Published in the United States by Random House, Inc. New York, and simultaneously in Canada by Random House of Canada Limited, Toronto, Canada.

Library of Congress Catalog Card Number: 82-90504

ISBN: 0-345-32012-3

Cover designed by Brian Strater and Mike Fentz
Manufactured in the United States of America

First Edition: October 1982

CRASH!!!
SQUAWK!

YEOW!!

COME HERE, HONEY BUN, COME TO DADDY

WHAT'S THE MATTER, HONEY BUN? DID THAT MEAN OLD CAT AND DOG NEXT DOOR TRY TO HURT YOU AGAIN?

I THOUGHT SO

WELL, JUST LOOK AT YOU, HUBERT... POTTED AGAIN! HEH, HEH, HEH, HEH

DAGNABBIT, REBA, CAN'T YOU SEE I'VE BEEN ASSAULTED BY THOSE PESKY VARMINTS. BRING ME THE PHONE!

YOU'VE DONE IT THIS TIME! I'M GOING TO FIX YOUR WAGONS ONCE AND FOR ALL!!

HELLO, CITY POUND? THIS IS HUBERT ON MAIN STREET. I'VE GOT A COUPLE OF CUSTOMERS FOR YOU

SEND A TRUCK RIGHT OVER

WHAT TOOK YOU SO LONG?

RHETT, RHETT.
WHATEVER
SHALL I DO?
WHEREVER
SHALL I GO?

TAKE ME TO YOUR
LEADER, EARTHLING,
OR I'LL ATOMIZE
YOUR FACE

PTUI

WELL, IF IT ISN'T
NATURE'S MOST
PERFECT FOOD...

I'M BORED, BORED-BORED-BORED-BORED-BORED-BORED-BORED-BORED. I AM BORED

THAT'S IT! I'M GOING DOWN TO THE CITY POUND AND I'M GOING TO BREAK ODIE OUT OF THERE!

LOOK OUT, POUND! HERE COMES GARFIELD!

DON'T WORRY, OLD BUDDY, YOU'LL BE OKAY

WELL, I SUPPOSE YOU BOYS HAD A BIG NIGHT, SINGING ON THE FENCE AND CHASING CARS

WHILE I SAT HOME AND WORRIED MYSELF SICK OVER YOU

I THOUGHT SO

OH, VERY WELL, GARFIELD

An Interview with **Garfield**

Q: Garfield, congratulations on the success of your first television special! How do you feel?

A: Hungry!

Q: Do you think success has gone to your head?

A: It's hard to be humble when you're as great as I am.

Q: Why wasn't there any sex and violence in your special?

A: Nobody's perfect.

Q: How do you feel about commercials?

A: Too long to sit through; too short for a trip to the sandbox.

Q: Do you have any further comments?

A: Where's my Emmy?

JIM DAVIS